Lario Sinigaglia

THE NEGATION

Youcanprint *Self – Publishing*

Title | The Negation
Author | Ilario Sinigaglia
ISBN | 978-88-93215-33-6

Youcanprint Self-Publishing
Via Roma, 73 – 73039 Tricase (LE) – Italy
www.youcanprint.it
info@youcanprint.it
Facebook: face book.com/youcanprint.it
Twitter: twitter.com/youcanprintit

PREFACE

The subject of the book is a descent into the depth and the intelligence of the language, especially of natural language.

And it is also the suggestion of an explanation of an aspect of natural intelligence that seems to consist of an appropriate use of the logical contradiction.

But nothing about all this could exist if "the negation" did not exist, as the book will gradually try to explain. The negation is really well-known to us: it is the logical operator that inverts the value of truth of a sentence into something like "it is not true".

So it is nothing that is not well-known to a speaking child, yet it is a spark from where an enormous fire starts: the real fire of Prometheus.

We speak of paradoxes but this is just to show the intelligence of the language that, through a paradox, points out an abuse of the language and of cognitive discard. This last one could be defined as the unknown background of every language.

So we also speak of general rules for a correct use of the language, those which are above the merely grammatical rules. As a matter of fact a sentence which is grammatically correct can equally be an abuse of the language.

Finally a suggestion to the reader: the book is addressed to readers who are not experts and it contains the necessary explanations to go on reading. In spite of this, you cannot understand everything at once, here or somewhere else. Those who want to understand everything before going on, will simply not go on. Go on then and you will certainly understand more, if not everything. This simple yet courageous rule has guided me both in my readings and in my writings.

CHAPTER ONE
THE COGNITIVE TWINS

Let Alfa and Beta be two twin brothers who are extraordinarily united in the existential experience. They make up together a cognitive unity that never separates yet it has its own functions divided within itself. They communicate using natural languages and this way their cognitive course is marked out by their conversations.

Their role is different: Alfa reveals "facts", communicates them to Beta who registers them in his memory.

Only Alfa has access to the facts and he communicates every revealed fact to Beta.

Beta registers the facts as they have been communicated to her by Alfa and if necessary she elaborates them again operating inferences of an exclusively deductive kind, but she has no access to the facts.

Alfa has access to Beta's memory.

All that Beta possesses and administers is all the beliefs of the couple.

Alfa and Beta are human and therefore not all the beliefs of the couple depend on Alfa's communications, but there is an original heritage which has been communicated by their Parents, if we broadly speak. This original heritage we mentioned was communicated genetically or culturally, we suppose, out of simplicity, once for all.

Genetic communication has got an implicit form and the cultural has got an explicit one.

An implicit knowledge is the one you have outside your awareness. As a matter of fact the twins have "handled" objects long before knowing the meaning of the word "handling".

An explicit knowledge is given using the language or exemplifying the behavior.

This set of original knowledge that certainly exists and that is not really given "once and for all" (human beings are instructed for years but also a lot of animal species instruct their children) is useful to prove that the further knowledge, acquired by the cognitive couple, has a differential nature. It means they are variations of an initial heritage that the Species and Society have invested in the individuals forming the cognitive couple.

This investment, from the point of view of the Species and of Society, is often a failure. But few individuals are enough to make it a very good investment as they increase its value.

You can find a similar logic in those funds that invest in the *start-ups*, the new firms which have to realize new ideas: few are successful, but the successful ones have enormous profits.

CHAPTER TWO
THE BELIEFS

First of all we observe that we can have beliefs only if we think they are true. Obviously Alfa and Beta are aware they have had also false beliefs, yet what constitutes the present heritage of beliefs is considered true.

Alfa and Beta, perhaps unaware, are Popper's followers: they believe that a belief is true only until they have proof of the opposite, that is till it proves false. At that point it becomes a false belief and it means it is no longer a belief. They know that in the past people thought some entities existed yet they did not, like the planetary system of Ptolemy, an astronomer of ancient times who thought the Earth was in the center of the universe, so that planets and stars, the Sun included, rotated round it. Or like the philosophical stone which was considered capable of transforming all metals into gold by alchemists.

They too do not believe in Father Christmas any longer and have painfully learnt that some people, who were considered friends, were not in reality; that lovers who were considered faithful, were not in reality; that investments, which were considered safe, have proved to be failures.

Yet this is not a good reason to give up having beliefs.

As a matter of fact how is it possible to have none?

We need to say precisely that falsified beliefs cease to exist for this reason but they are preserved, in Beta's memory, classified like mistakes and also as painful experiences. Yet they make up a particular heritage, called experience that is considered as more useful for the future as harder it was achieved in the past.

Mistakes are a variegated forest we will deal with in the future.

The entities and the relationships which make up the heritage of the beliefs of Alfa and Beta, are without doubts considered as existent. They believe in the Laws of Physics and also of Good Luck, which is what the winners of superlottery have. Till now they have had no Good Luck, that is it has not knocked at their door though it can do that in the future. Good Luck exists though it is not present. This is not strange: they have had ancestors who are no longer alive. Jinx and astral Influences do not exist instead, they are not one of their beliefs but just other people's belief which they know it is false and they call it superstition.

We notice that for Alfa and Beta the falsified beliefs are all past, while those that are thought true are all present. The future ones do not exist and cannot exist, as the memories of the future do not exist. Yet we believe they will exist, even this is a belief as much as the future memories will exist.

The beliefs are also a variegated forest we classify like this:

a)   Ontological Beliefs concerning the existence of entities and their qualities and relationships;

b)   Epistemic Beliefs if the methods used for what you learn from what is in a) and its value are concerned;

c)   Linguistic Beliefs if the languages we use to speak about what is in a) and b) are concerned.

All this is part of man's tendency to classify which is not harmful as far as an ontological value is given to it. As a matter of fact it is difficult to separate the entities from the knowledge we have of them, while the language and its expressions are in turn entities, the language deals with, as we will see.

Finally the border, if it really exists, between beliefs and knowledge is vague, unless we admit that "knowledge" is the name we give to our own beliefs and "beliefs" is the name given to others' knowledge.

CHAPTER THREE
THE FACTS

A *Fact* is all that modifies the current system of beliefs. This definition shows that a fact is as relative to a system of beliefs as much as to the time when it is revealed. And it has a differential nature because it is made into a fact just because it diverges from the beliefs in force and for this reason it is different from what Alfa expects. When Alfa finds a fact, he pronounces a sentence which has an *ontological predicate*. It is as if saying that when Alfa notices a fact, he finds the existence of an entity or of a category of entities or their qualities, which had not been foreseen by the system of beliefs in force and then it can modify these same ones.

During our conceptual experiment Alfa pronounces only ontological sentences and he communicates them to Beta.

Facts may have a different nature and may be, for example, *events* if they are independent from the cognitive couple.

They are *acts* if they are done by the cognitive couple as an act of initiation: an exam, an oath, a meaningful choice.

They are *learnings* if they have an epistemic value and they vary the knowledge of the cognitive couple.

Even Beta can pronounce sentences but this happens very rarely because, in any case, what Beta says cannot change the system of beliefs of the cognitive couple.

Beta can pronounce infinite sentences and all of them rigorously *true* at the light of the system of beliefs in force. But she does not tell them as they are obvious. The real function that Beta has is remembering and sometimes refusing a fact suggested by Alfa. Beta is the keeper of a heritage of beliefs and she tends to minimize its variations. Instead Alfa tends to maximize the variations and this is the reason why the cognition requires the cognitive couple.

We notice that facts constitute a *totally ordered set* as a fact is relative to a state of beliefs and this depends on the previous fact which determined it.

In short: each fact could correspond to an ordinal number (first, second ..... nth, a term defining any successive ordinal) and as ordinals are totally well ordered by the relationship "<" which towards right means *bigger* and so towards left means *smaller*, then also facts can be ordered with the same relationship. When facts are ordered this way they form a *succession* which is said to be totally *ordered* as, if you take by chance two facts included in the succession, one of the two is *smaller*, the other is *bigger*, which means they are respectively *previous* and *successive*.

We notice that facts can be totally ordered, but, in general, not all the entities can be ordered this way. Yet often the total order is considered desirable because people try to apply it even by mistake.

Think about the election of *Miss Italy* where a hundred wonderful girls have to be put in a succession from the first (Miss Italy) to the hundredth, in order of their beauty. But their beauty depends also on their movements, expressions, and so on. In short, a jury of experts of female beauty establishes, by voting, with some majority principle, such a succession of beauties that, if the jury changes, the succession would almost certainly be different.

What is left is the disappointment for so much beauty so sadly exhibited, concentrated and therefore underestimated. You find the hundredth is the one who would arouse the interest in every village.

CHAPTER FOUR
THE MISTAKES

"Life is a succession of mistakes. No mistakes, no life". It is an aphorism of Ennio Flaiano.

Alfa and Beta promise not to make mistakes, for the future, but, if they look back, they have to admit that Flaiano's words have a disturbing depth.

A succession of mistakes suggests that the original heritage of beliefs contains some mistakes, and not few. And even more: that the cultural part of Alfa and Beta's education has not identified and removed them, but has even confirmed and accentuated them.

It is true that the human species is young, if other living species are considered, actually it has lived for hundreds of generations. That is it has accumulated enough experience to identify probable mistakes of its own heritage of beliefs.

The question is not new and it goes back at least to the Greek tragedies of the V century B.C.

Giacomo Leopardi, in the Poem dedicated to Silvia, still asks himself this.

"... Che pensieri soavi,
che speranze, che cori, o
Silvia mia!
Quale allor ci apparia
la vita umana e il fato!
Quando sovviemmi di cotanta
speme,
un affetto mi preme
acerbo e sconsolato,
e tornami a doler di mia
sventura.
O natura, o natura,
perché non rendi poi
quel che prometti allor?
perché di tanto
inganni i figli tuoi? ..."

*"... What sweet thoughts,
what hopes, what choirs, my
Silvia!
How then appeared to us
human life and destiny
When I remember such a
hope
an affection awakes
bitter and desolate
and I start again to complain
about my bad luck
nature, nature
why don't you give back then
what you have promised?
Why do you deceive your
children so much? ...."*

Why not only nature, but also parents, successively, deceive their children?
Alfa and Beta give themselves an answer that the mistakes, that are usually called illusions later, correspond to betrayed hopes.
Leopardi again:

"Anche peria fra poco
la speranza mia dolce: agli
anni miei
anche negaro i fati
la giovinezza. Ahi come,
come passata sei,
cara compagna dell'età mia
nova, mia
lacrimata speme!"

"also my sweet hope
dies soon misfortune
denied my years
my youth. Ahi, how
how you have passed,
you the dear fellow of my
new age
my hope in tears!"

The species of Alfa and Beta is yet young, but none had more hopes and more disappointments. Yet Beta memorizes the mistakes and not the successes. The first and not the second are experience.

The fairy tales, dedicated to children, are factories of illusions, so that K. Kerenyi, the great scholar of Greek myth, observed that fairy tales deny what myth affirms.

Then between the two narrations there is not that contiguity that is sometimes supposed.

Alfa and Beta come to the conclusion that the mistakes of initial information can be really defined illusions.

They are usually a disaster for the individual, yet they are providential for the species that receives a loan it will not refund.

States and their collectors do the same.

When Alfa communicates a fact to Beta he uses dry sentences which affirm the presence or the absence of entities or that they have or do not have certain properties or relationships.

Even presence and absence are properties after all. But they are properties of what exists.

They never discuss about the absolute existence af entities and their properties, because they could not speak about something that has no kind of existence. Even a baseless belief exists exactly as such.

Then they observe the language they use and precisely the predicates that Alfa uses which we could then define *ontological*.

Beta instead uses some predicates which we could define *tautological* on the whole, because they do not communicate *facts* but implications of facts which have been previously recorded.

Here is the result of some observations you will draw conclusions from, that is facts.

They are of Venetian origin, though they spent most part of their existence in Crema, that is in Lombardy. Crema is a small beautiful town of the *lowlands* (Lombardy is implied). The *lowlands* start from the area of the springs where Alpine waters come to surface because the permeable gravels end, brought to the valley by prehistoric glaciers and the base of the plain emerges, made up of impermeable clays: an ancient sea bottom.

The area surrounding Crema is a prosperous countryside dotted with villages, in each of them distinguishable variations of Crema dialect are spoken. In the north you can hear influences from Bergamo, in the east from Brescia, in the south from Cremona (that is proto-Emilian) and so on. It is a question of cadence and of pronunciation rather than a difference of terms and so you can understand even when people speak Italian. This choir constitutes the linguistic area of Crema and Alfa and Beta, with a marked venetian cadence, everybody is aware of, are outside the choir.

Crema, about 34,000 inhabitants, has a population which is basically stable of number and of fact: most of them were born in Crema from parents from Crema. So not all of them know each other but they know people who know strangers and their parents and the various parental ramifications. Some families in view are *well known* by everybody.

If not everybody knows each other, at least everybody sees each other, especially those who attend public events, have a walk in Mazzini street, where everybody walked, at least when they were young, because there you can find shops (in the past there were no hypermarkets) and above all because there girls go for a walk. It is a shared opinion that there it is nice to see.

So an inhabitant of Crema who has always seen people go around Crema (like Alfa or Beta) has the reliable belief that they are from Crema, especially if they have a deceitful ancestor in the person of an acquired aunt from Crema or of a famous mayor, with the same surname of the father, yet neither a distant relative.

One day Alfa and Beta speak to a gentleman from Crema (we can call him "Eta") and he is ready to observe: "You aren't from Crema, are you?". The Venetian cadence betrays them.

We notice: "you are not from Crema!", this is what people say to those who had previously thought they were from Crema. As a matter of fact Eta is a well-known wanderer, who has never thought of telling the inhabitants of Beijing or of Calcutta that they are not from Crema, though this was perfectly true.

Let us imagine now that Eta goes to Central Africa and there he runs into *a potasaying person.*

Let us open a parenthesis: *pota* is a word used in eastern Lombardy. Certainly in the past it meant the female (sexual) organ. Now no longer so, at least in Crema.

Perhaps still in the area of Brescia where hardworking friendly people still live, though they are a little *material.* This characteristic is shown in the realism of Lombard painting which is missing in the Venetian as if the Mincio was a border of the soul. In Crema, then, *pota* is not a stock phrase to fill silence like *therefore* or the English word *well,* but it is a term capable to express any feeling, as long as it is correctly well-tuned, something only the inhabitants of Crema are able to do, so they can be defined *potasaying.*

I am more precise: even the term *thing* can be referred to anything but as it lacks a demonstrative sign, it does not refer to it. *Pota* instead not only indicates but also shows, exhibits and represents any communicable feeling and it also lends itself to rhetorical artifices. As a matter of fact *pota* can be introductory/explicative, gloomily fatalist, rhetorical/sarcastic, pathetic, irascible, affectionate, conspiratorial, impulsively affirmative, doubtful, apologetic and even more (see the special study wiktionary.org/wiki), yet only if you are from Crema.

Eta then runs into an African who had spent a long time with a missionary from Crema, from whom he had learnt the right use of *pota.*

Eta then runs towards the African, embraces him and exclaims: "You are from Crema" surprised to meet one in central Africa.

We notice *you are from Crema* is what you say to a person who was not previously thought to be as such and you never say that to the usual people from Crema, though this is perfectly true.

Now we have to put our ideas in order but not without noticing that there is an analogy between the cognitive process of Eta and the one that Alfa and Beta develop in the couple: the attention is given to the exception and not to the rule.

Besides this the exceptions seem to be made up of particular negations, which, just as to say, are internal to the predicate. There will be the moment when we have to refine the concept. For the moment we observe that Alfa and Beta are *not from Crema* in a different way from the inhabitants of Beijing. They are, in a sense, *inhabitants of Crema but not from Crema.*

CHAPTER SIX
CATEGORIC SENTENSES ON WEDDING DRESSES

Alfa and Beta have been invited to a wedding ceremony of two young couple. They are waiting for the bride's arrival at the church square. The bride's car arrives, with the usual delay, she gets out slowly, hindered by her long dress and by its train. "The dress is not white" Alfa immediately observes. A lot of the people present whisper the same thing. Actually the dress is pale winter blue, but this does not seem to be important. It could also be light green but what counts is that *the dress is not white*. It is the *not white* dress of a young bride, yet all young brides wear a white dress.

Alfa and Beta had heard about underwater wedding ceremony and also about motorcyclist wedding.

The young bride was wearing the diving suit and also the suit track and nobody thought that they were a wedding dress.

But in this case what does Beta register?

As a matter of fact there are two opportunities:

1)   A light-blue dress is not a wedding dress (as it is not the diving suit), so nothing modifies the beliefs in force and so nothing is registered.

2)   In this case a light-blue dress is considered a wedding dress. So at least a light-blue wedding dress exists and this is a fact we should register.

Yet this is not only a fact that could be isolated, like an infective person in forty days.

Actually "All wedding dresses are white" and "at least one not white wedding dress exists" are two sentences that, taken together, are contradictory.

The "and" put between the two sentences is a logical conjunction with sign "$\wedge$", whose meaning is that the two sentences have a joint value of truth and, in this case, the value is *true* only if both the joint sentences are true. Yet in this case the sentences cannot be both true.

(Note: two joint sentences with a sign "V", the logical disjunction, have a *true* value if only at least one of the two is true. The negation with a "¬" sign inverts the value of truth of a sentence and then it transforms the *true* value into the *false* value and vice versa).

The fact that this is the natural logic is proved by the fact that the people present said: *the wedding dress is not white* (as expected, as it should have been), and they did not say: *the wedding dress is light-blue*. Actually whether it is light-blue or pale green it is irrelevant. A more definite color would have created more bewilderment. The black color would not have been accepted. The bridegroom's mother would have failed, a lot of guests would have left.

Let us observe then that clothes of pastel color can be *not white*, while a black dress is just black and that is all. It is a mournful dress the one that the bride could, or better should, wear at her husband's funeral.

But let us go back to Beta. If Beta chooses the second opportunity, that is: *at least one light-blue wedding dress exists*, she is obliged to modify the belief *all the wedding dresses are white* in the belief *that all wedding dresses are white or light-blue.*

We notice then that Beta has a task of selection of information we had not understood before. She eliminates every contradiction of her beliefs, but she has two ways to do that, and that is:

1)   She denies that the light-blue dress is for the bride;

2)   She modifies and extends the concept of the wedding dress to light-blue wedding dresses.

In the second case the cognitive couple's beliefs change, but the world changes too. Actually at the next wedding, if the young bride has a light-blue dress, this will not certainly be a fact.

Then Beta eliminates the contradictions which might be in the concepts (intensions), generating only extensions which are not contradictory. Yet Beta has two ways to do it, one of which is conservative and one is modifying the beliefs.

Let us limit ourselves, for the moment, to notice that, while the extensions are defined rigidly, the intensions are instead intrinsically ductile and this is a characteristic which allows Beta's choice.

It allows but it is not binding: as a matter of fact Beta's choice is arbitrary, though it is influenced by the habits of the family and of society (which can be mutually divergent).

Let us admit it: we had not understood that silent Beta was so important.

CHAPTER SEVEN
PROBABILISTIC PREDICATES

Alfa and Beta have not only beliefs but also knowledge of a different nature. Like conjectures, hypothesis, evaluations. It is an uncertain knowledge because they are badly known states of things or even unknowable because inaccessible in the present and, to a greater extent, if they are put in the past or in the future.

It is that kind of knowledge where adverbs come first like *probably* or *likely* in sentences of an hypothetic kind.

An unpleasant fact leads them to these considerations.

In a small domestic poultry pen they rear four laying young hens, they are fond of and which supply daily eggs to their kitchen: Altea, Berenice, Calipso and Dafne.

One morning Alfa enters the poultry pen and exclaims: "A hen is missing!".

As a matter of fact only three were in the poultry pen.

There was a hole under the fence, probably dug by the thief. Certainly not dug by the hen, that was a laying Paduan race.

But who was the thief? A fox? A dog? Perhaps their own dog Fido?

Would Fido be a thief or at least a slothful keeper?

In any case a fact was certain: their belief to have four hens had dissolved in front of the fact that the hens now were three. And they could not be certain also about this for the future, as a thief was at work, whose identity had not been ascertained for the moment.

But what does *"a hen is missing"* mean? In the bathroom of one's house there is none, yet nobody had never said that one was missing and still less four.

Then the hens can be only in the poultry or they can be missing. Moreover if the hens are four, more than four cannot be missing. But what is the difference between one poultry pen with three hens and another with four hens, where one is missing?

Alfa and Beta decide to think about a suitable notation to represent their event.

If you call the four hens "**a, b, c, d**" (from the initials of their names), they should have made the following hypothesis:

1)   All of them are there and that is: {a,b,c,d}. The braces indicate that the hens are the elements of a set which, in the mind, has the same function of the poultry pen: it contains them. In practice the thought of a fence contains thought of the hens.

2)   One is missing and therefore, as one of the four hens can be missing, there might be these situations: {b,c,d}, {a,c,d}, {a,b,d}, {a,b,c}.

3)   Two are missing and then: {a,b}, {a,c}, {a,d}, {b,c}, {b,d}, {c,d}.

4)   Three are missing and then only one is left: {a}, {b}, {c}, {d}.

5)   All of them are missing: (Damn!) and then how can I write it? *Zero* is not right. Even in the bathroom there are zero hens, yet none is missing. So Alfa and Beta will write: {Øa, Øb, Øc, Ød}. The symbol "Ø" indicates *deficiency*, which is specified by putting the name of the missing hen close to the right.

With an easy extension of the use of "Ø", they insert them also into the other sets where hens are missing (for example {a,b,c,Ød} into the set where Dafne is missing, (the stolen hen). But they do not insert it into the set where there are all the hens, which they will call, for this reason, **reference set**, which is the one you use to measure what is missing.

Alfa and Beta have by then got off and they consult a small handbook of calculus of probability where they find out that the probability of the event consisting of two independent events is the product of probability of each (I launch a coin: the probability to obtain head is ½, that is 50%, then the probability to obtain *head* twice in two launches is ½ x ½ = ¼).

They think (in a first approximation) that the probability of the theft of each hen is 50% (that is ½) every night and that each theft is an independent event from the others (in the handbook *stochastically independent* is written).

They know that if they enter the poultry pen the following day they cannot have the naive belief they will find four hens there, but they will have to admit that one (and only one) of the sixteen situations previously advanced, each of them consisting of four elementary events (each hen is there or it is not there), each of them has the probability-product of the four elementary probabilities and that is ½ x ½ x ½ x ½ = 1/16. They will call this exhaustive set of events: **space of events**.

And precisely the calculations were valuable for the past, as today Dafne is already missing.

(you will see later that the space of events is one of the interpretations of an aggregate we will call **Ur**, that is **universe relative to a property**).

I say! There are 16 events and each of them has a probability of 1/16, so the sum of probabilities is equal to 1. That "**1**" reminds them that 100% of probabilities they attribute to a reliable fact. It is not a chance: actually the 16 events we examined are all the possible events and therefore one of them will happen and on it will collapse the whole castle of probabilities, as it will become the unique reliable event (probability 100% that is **1**) of the sixteen hypothesized reliable events.

Are there also events with a probability 0%? Certainly: the impossible ones, like stealing five hens when there are just four.

Alfa and Beta start having the disturbing thought that at every expectancy of theirs (and therefore belief) a probability should be associated.

Can it be possible that Fido doesen't welcome them when it sees them again?

They cannot believe it.

They notice that the collapse of the hypothesis which are mutually incompatible and entirely exhaustive in a single realized fact is worth as well eliminating the contradiction which exists when you connect the hypothesis forming the space of events (as a matter of fact the hens are there or they are missing!).

So there is an analogy between a predicate asserting the realization of an *aleatory* fact (it means *uncertain*) and the lack of realization of the other aleatory facts which made up the space of events, and those predicate which eliminate the contradiction from the sentences examined in chapter 6).

Yet while those eliminate the contradiction of propositions, this latter eliminates the contradiction of events.

The first could be defined the contradictions of the subject and so subjective, while the second could be defined contradictions of the events and then objective.

But also *intensional* contradictions the first and *estensional* contradictions the second.

What is the relation between the two contradictions?

We can then synthetize like that: the elimination of the intensional contradiction is primary as they identify facts that can be potentially valid and therefore can be included in the space of events. Successfully the possible facts will collapse into a realized fact and the estensional contradiction will be eliminated.

The cognitive background

The elimination of the intensional contradiction implies the discard of a present or potential truth, the subject will not take

into account of in the future and it will be his **cognitive background.**
Such a discard is legitimate and valid only if the discarded truth is not relevant.

CHAPTER EIGHT
CONCEPT AND ENDOCONCEPTUAL NEGATION

CATEGORICAL SENTENCES

Now it is advisable to meditate about Alfa and Beta's experiences.

We will do it using an old but valid instrument of Aristotle: the categorical propositions. They affirm that, given a category of individuals, **existent for hypothesis,** each has a certain characteristic or *nobody* has got it. And also that *some* (with the meaning of *at least one*) have a certain characteristic or, in alternative, they have got none.

1)   Universal affirmative sentence: "all individuals of **s** type have property **B**"

And formally: $\forall x \, [s(x) \rightarrow B(x)]$.

"**x**" is an individual variable, "**s**" a type of individuals, "**B**" is a property.

In the interpretation which interests us **s** represents the *wedding dresses* and **B** the property of *being white* which is (for Alfa and Beta) the characteristic of every wedding dress.

The formula represents the natural language and the signs "$\forall$" and "$\exists$" mean respectively for "each" and "at least one exists" referred to the variable (in the example "x") and they are defined "universal quantifier" and "existential quantifier". Yet we have to state that the literal translation of the formula is: *every s individual has the B property* and later the importance of this difference between the natural language and the formal one will emerge.

Making it simpler in the natural language: *all wedding dresses are white.*

We notice that the quantifiers transform a propositional form into a proposition and that only the proposition, if it is interpreted, has a meaning and then it may be true or false.

2)   Negative universal proposition: "no individual of **s** type has got property **B**".

Formally: $\forall x\, [s(x) \rightarrow \neg B(x)]$.

We observe that the negative universal proposition should be translated by the formula like that: *each s individual has got property **not B***. Yet the natural language would normally interpret like this: *no wedding dress is white*.

Have a look now at the particular sentences.

3)   Particular affirmative propositions: "Some **s** individuals have got property **B**."

Formally: $\exists(x)[s(x) \wedge B(x)]$.

Translation of the formula: *There are some s individuals* (at least one) *who have got property **B***.

The interpretation says: *some of the wedding dresses are white*.

4)   Particular negative proposition: "Some **s** individuals have not got **B** property".

Formally: $\exists(x)[s(x) \wedge \neg B(x)$.

Translation of the formula: *there are some s individuals* (at least one) *who have got **not B** property* which is interpreted: *some wedding dresses are not white*.

The Medieval logical named the affirmative propositions 1 and 3 respectively "A" and "I" from: **AFFIRMO** and the negative propositions 2 and 4 respectively "E" and "O" from : **NEGO**. The use has been preserved and then it will be ours.

We are interested to join the propositions of A and O type (1 and 4) and those of E and I type (2 and 3) that is $\mathbf{A \wedge O}$ e $\mathbf{E \wedge I}$ that are said to be **reciprocally contradictory.**

(The sign "∧" is the logical joint between two sentences; therefore it forms a third proposition which is true if both propositions are true).

The reciprocally contradictory propositions have got this important characteristic: if one is true then the other is false (and vice versa). Therefore their joint is a **contradiction**, that is a proposition which is, on the whole, always false, whatever **s** individuals and **B** properties.

As a direct consequence their disjunction (A∨O e E∨I) is always true and therefore a **tautology**.

(The "∨" sign is the logical disjunction between the two propositions; therefore it forms a third proposition which is true if at least one of the two propositions is true. The examples will make the concept clearer).

Formally:

$$A \wedge O = \forall x \, [s(x) \rightarrow B(x)] \wedge \exists x \, [s(x) \wedge \neg B(x)]$$

The proposition (A∧O) is defined "PAT", that is "total affirmative predicate", while (E∧I) is defined "PNT" that is "total negative predicate".

Translation: every **s** individual has got **B** property and at least one **s** individual exists with **non-B** property.

(To simplify we do not deal with (E∧I) for the moment as the arguments we developed further for (A∧O) would be analogous for (E∧I). Moreover the affirmative propositions are more frequent than the negative ones).

Obviously it is a contradictory proposition. To understand its nature we need to examine its extension.

We define {**B**} the set of all **s** individuals, who have **B** property and we define {**ØB**} the set of all the individuals of **s** type who have **non-B** property.

There are the following relationships:

a)   {B}∪ {ØB}= {B} and

b)   {B}∩ {ØB} = {ØB}

Obviously if **all** the individuals of **s** type have **B** property, there is none who have non-B property and so {B} and {ØB} have no element in common as {ØB} is an empty set. Yet, in the interpretation we will give of them, {ØB} is not a banally empty set, but a set where all elements present in its reference set are missing, that is in {B}.

Then the set union of {B} with the empty set gives as a result set {B} while the intersection of {B} with the empty set {ØB} gives as a result the empty set. This results respectively from a) and b).

(The signs "∪" and "∩" indicate respectively the set union and the set intersection, practicable operations on sets. The set resulting from the union contains [just once] every element contained in one or the other of the joined sets. The set resulting from the intersection contains [just once] every element contained in both the intersected sets).

Let us go back to PAT which is a contradictory sentence as it is the result of the union of two sentences which are reciprocally contradictory, so both cannot be true, and let us give them a meaning.

PAT affirms that every individual of **s** type has **B** property and that at least one individual of **s** type exists with **non-B** property.

We believe that PAT affirms (predicates) a property of **every s** individual in the first part (the universal affirmative proposition) and a property of **all s** individuals in its whole, affirming then that there are individuals (at least one) of **s** type which have the **non-B** property.

But as soon as we interpret we understand that this is just another way of saying that there are **wedding dresses which are not white**. And just the contradiction exhibits the semantic power of natural language.

PAT exists, but it lasts for a short time like a particle of antimatter which happened in a universe of matter, very soon it annihilates, in a lighting of light. Yet that lighting is what shows that the human mind does not act recursively and it is for this reason different from a machine (though a machine, that is a *computer*, has often superior performances to those of the mind in the recursive tasks, that is the mechanic ones, that are proper of it).

THE DECISION: ELIMINATION OF THE CONTRADICTION OF "PAT"

Let us go back to the cognitive couple.
When Alfa announces: "the wedding dress is not white" Beta has two alternatives:
I.   Beta, basing himself on the system of beliefs in force, that is *all wedding dresses are white*, **deduces** that *the light-blue dress, the brides wears,* **is not a wedding dress**. This choice, that we can define conservative, because it preserves the beliefs in force, implies that Alfa's announcement, *the wedding dress is not white*, does not concern a *fact*.
We had previously stated that Alfa had to announce only *facts*, such are just those which modify the system of beliefs in force. Then Alfa should not have announced anything and Beta, the one who is usually silent, informs Alfa this way.
Therefore Beta decides that PAT should be interpreted in such a way that the second part of the formula is $\not\exists x\,[s(x) \wedge \neg B(x)]$ that is PAT becomes:
$$\forall(x)[s(x) \to B(x)] \wedge \not\exists(x)\,[s(x) \wedge \neg B(x)]$$
(the sign "$\not\exists$", that is the existential barred quantifier denies the quantifier and it means *no x exists*. The use of the bar is frequent also in other cases and of an intuitive meaning).
We will name this formula "P1" (first predicate).
Translation: *Every **s** has **B** property and there is no **s** that has* **non-B** *property.*

And interpreting P 1 we can conclude: *All wedding dresses are white and no wedding dress exists that is not white*. Therefore we are taken back to an analogous situation to that of the brides who wear the diving suit or the tracksuit of the motorist.

II.   Beta accepts that Alfa has communicated a fact. In this case the fact is the one communicated in the second part of PAT, or that *at least a wedding dress exists that is not white*, and this is precisely the light-blue dress, that the bride wears. We notice that the dress which is *not white* is not a dress of any color different from white, but a dress whose color is such that it is acceptable as a bride's dress. From the example we made in chapter 6) we had reached the conclusion that, perhaps, any pastel color would be acceptable for a bride's dress and it could be then *not white*. But a violent color would not be acceptable and, in particular, the black color is not conceivable as it is a mournful color and therefore it is impossible that a wedding dress is black, as a wedding is a joyful event.

But even in this second case the contradiction of PAT must be resolved, as our mind elaborates the contradictions and, doing that, it eliminates them. The contradictions exist, but only before the formation of the sentence. Actually the formation of the sentence consists in the elimination of the contradiction.

In this case Beta modifies its own beliefs and, **from now on**, she will think that *dresses are all **white or light- blue***. But it is clear that being *white or light-blue* is a different property from *being white*. Therefore if *being white* was the property called **B**, the new property could be called **B V C** that is *white or light-blue*.

After this interpretation PAT becomes:

$$\forall(x)\{s(x) \rightarrow [\, B(x) \vee C(x)]\}$$

Which we define P 2 (second predicate)

(the "V" sign indicates disjunction, that is the property white or light-blue, while the "Λ" sign would indicate *white and simultaneously light-blue*, which is contradictory, that is not existent).

It is worth making some observations:

A.   P 1 and P 2 are sentences which define the properties of two sets of wedding dresses. The sets, which are the extensions of the sentences are different (that is {B} e {B∪C}) because the properties (B e B∨C) defining them are different. These sets contain every individual of **s** type who has **B** properties or **B∨C** properties. But *every* individual does not mean *all individuals*. An intension exists which picks up *all* individuals and it is precisely PAT whose extension is not a set but an **Ur, or the aggregate which contains all the individuals who have B and non-B properties**, as you will see later.

B.   The PAT formula is contradictory and so is Ur aggregate because it contains sets which are reciprocally incompatible. The nature of this incompatibility will be made clearer later but it is analogous to the one we saw in chapter 7) when we spoke about probabilistic predicates. As a matter of fact there an Ur was the aggregate containing all the possible events, but, in the example in question, each event was incompatible with every other event. So the Ur aggregate of the possible events could collapse only in one of the possible events. The analogy with Ur, which is the representation of PAT, consists of this: **PAT can collapse only in one of the predicates which have defined P 1 and P2**.

And which of the two depends on one of Beta's arbitrary choices. The choice is arbitrary because it does not depend on acquired beliefs or on rules of the language or on rules of logic. Instead it depends on **choices of value** which are Beta's personal choices, possibly accepted by her own social group. If you want to make PAT not contradictory you have to associate each of the elementary proposition it is composed a percentage included between 0 and 1 and such that the sum of two percentages is "1". Yet what do the percentages intuitively measure? Obviously Alfa and Beta have to choose between P 1 and P 2, as there is no middle course. Each guest to the wedding will have to do the same. But not everybody will choose in the same way. Then the percentages associated to each PAT proposition indicate the way how the guests' judgement is divided up about the fact that the dress the bride is wearing is or is not a wedding dress. If the guests were interrogated about it, one certain percentage would choose P 1 and another P 2 (% P 1 + % P 2 = 100 %).

If these percentages would have been correctly valued a priori and they would have been attributed to each of proposition which make up PAT, the same PAT could be interpreted as a predition of opinions. **Yet it is obvious that the same divergence of opinions lies in the fact that PAT exists and it is made up of the conjunction of two contradictory propositions**.
C.   P 1 leaves Beta's beliefs unchanged. Instead P 2 changes Beta's beliefs and, therefore, P 2, if it exists, is necessarily successive to P 1 in the ordinal sense.

Yet the ordinal succession can be well interpreted as a temporal succession. In the succession of the predicates, that is the beliefs in force (the visions of reality) we understand perhaps the elusive nature of time. The one that clocks do not understand. As a matter of fact each system of beliefs in force contains every system of previous beliefs, though partially or totally falsified. After all we have a memory and we make experiences. We will speak about this later.
D.   The **endoconceptual** negation is set up against the **esoconceptual** negation.
There are then two negations: one internal to the concept and one external.

Let us make it clearer: in the given example the light-blue dress is *not white*, yet it is a wedding dress, in P 2 's interpretation.

While the light-blue dress is not a wedding dress in P 1 's interpretation.

ESOCONCEPTUAL AND ENDOCONCEPTUAL NEGATIONS

In practice there is no extension of the negation of a concept. That is to say that, given any concept, its pure negation, whose extension is the set of objects that *do **not** have the property which defines the members of a set,* constitutes such a vague aggregate that it has no practical relevance.

If we use the previous example, the P 1 aggregate does not put the light-blue dress into an absurd set of objects that would *not be wedding dresses* and therefore it could contain both shoes and tanks, but it puts the light-blue dress into the more useful set of women's clothes, which are not the bride's. Where actually it has always been: as a matter of fact P 1 's conservative choice consists of this.

P 2 predicate instead extends the set of wedding dresses and it restricts the set of women's dresses, which are not for the bride. It is therefore a collocation of the elements inside the set of women's dresses.

Yet as the set we are examining is that of wedding dresses, then P 1 denies that the light-blue dress is a part of it (esoconceptual negation), while P 2, admitting the *not white* dress of light-blue color among the wedding dresses constitutes an endoconceptual negation, which is relative to the set of wedding dresses.

Now, while a set is defined, a concept, for its nature, is not because it possesses a priori some potentialities of amplification or of reduction like those just examined.

The operation of reduction is simple, as it is a question of excluding from the extension of the concept well known elements, that were part of it previously.

The operation of amplification is instead complex, as it is a question of inserting into the extension set of the concept some elements which are indeterminate and which could even not be there at all.

In short any concept could have some potentialities which any set does not have, or must not have. In extension such potentialities are well represented by the "empty set" , when you attribute to it the capacity of representing those elements of a set which are "missing" if you consider a reference set. That is, those that are present in the complementary set, if you consider the reference set.

Even the reference set has its own complement it is expected that such complement is constituted by the elements missing from the reference set, that is by the lack of all the elements of the reference set.

That is by an empty set of elements and full of all the deficiencies.

This concept is not strange, on the contrary it is usual, just if you think of the bathroom and of the poultry pen of Alfa and Beta in chapter 7).

The small stolen hen is neither in the poultry pen nor in the bathroom. Yet it is missing in the poultry pen but it is not missing in the bathroom. Therefore in the poultry pen **there is** a missing hen, for example Dafne, that we have labelled $\{\emptyset d\}$.

The next step consists in representing, through the empty set, not only the lack of the elements which are *present now* in the reference set, but also the lack of those which are *potentially present* in the reference set, if enlarging the property defining it would be decided or if it should be done.

As far as what has been said is concerned, the empty set represents a potentiality.

Some potentialities are predictable, as the *successor* of any ordinal number. Other potentialities are unpredictable.

In turn unpredictability may have an *existential* or *quantitative* nature.

In the first case the existence itself of a new element is unpredictable, in the second case only its dimension, anyhow it is measured.

The aggregate representing the properties and its potentialities (that is every endoconceptual affirmation and negation) is defined **Ur**, that is relative Universe and it will be better examined later. For the moment it is worth observing that in the aggregate the complement set of every contained set is contained.

THE CONCEPT AND THE PROPERTY:

Now we make it clear what relation there is between *concept* and *property*: the concept identifies the property and nominates it, but it is not the property, yet just its name. The concept makes the property *treatable*, which in itself is only *predicable*, that is *referable* to individuals or to sets of individuals. This important distinction will be clearer later.

For the moment we underline the fact that the concept indicates the property but, in practice, it includes just some extensions and it cannot include them all. Then, operatively, that is in the practical linguistic use, the concept operates a subjective selection among the extensions that the property can include.

What are the consequences of this?

A dictionary is in practice a list of concepts, yet to each of them the speaker attributes one of his own meanings which might be shared with the cultural group it adheres to.

As a matter of fact the predication, as opposite to a concept, is used to clarify the particular meaning attributed to the concept.

But the meaning depends on a system of values, that is on an existential meaning, which overhangs and defines the meaning of a concept. And it is almost impossible to subvert the others' system of values because it is constituitive of the individual and very little stipulated.

Finally words do not have the same meaning for each speaker and this leads to vast consequences, like infinite explanations between lovers or like treatises and contracts differently interpreted by the parts. The same laws are variably interpreted by those who emanate them (Legislator) and by those who apply them (Court).

So the meaning of words is a battlefield of values in mutual conflict, with the opportunity to go too far and use strength.

PROBABILISTIC PREDICATES AND DETERMINED PREDICATES

If a predicate is ontological (that is not merely tautological) it may have a determined nature or a probabilistic nature.

It has a determined nature if it concerns an observation of the kind:

a) the fact is valid (or the individual exists). Let us remember, once more, that the existence we are speaking of is not absolute but only relative to the examined circumstances. You should then speak of "presence" or "absence" of what we are talking about.

b) the property we are talking about is verified or not verified considering the individuals we are talking about.

If instead the same affirmations are connoted by chance or uncertainty due to any reason (facts or entities recognizable with difficulty because remote, because hidden, because past or future), then the predicate has a probabilistic nature.

Yet in one case as in the other the representation of the predicate is necessarily an **Ur**, that is a *relative universe*.

Therefore a determinate ontological predicate coincides with the collapse of the total predicate (PAT) into a determined predicate of P1 or P2 type.

If instead a predicate concerns an event, which is an element of the set of possible events, then a probability is associated to the event. The whole of the possible events, that is an **Ur,** collapses then into the unique realized event.

We have already seen what relationship there is between the predicative collapse and the probabilistic collapse.

The preventive predicative collapse is necessary, as from this you obtain the individualization of facts to which, only later, it is possible to attribute a probability of occurrence.

THE TOTALITY

A simple predicative proposition is constituted by an entity (a thing, an individual, a set and later generically *individual*) whose property is affirmed or denied (that is predicated).

Every property is represented by an Ur, that is an aggregate that contains not only all the extensions of a certain property, but also the extensions of all the negations of the property itself, which we have defined *endoconceptual*.

In practice a concept catches not only all the individuals who have a certain property, but also those, only potential, who might have it.

The whole of all the individuals who have a certain property (**today**, that is *historically*) is the reference set and therefore the complementary set of the reference set is (**today**, that is *historically*) is an empty set, that is containing (today) the deficiencies of the elements contained in the reference set and potentially (that is tomorrow or in any case later) the presences of potential elements, individualized by the endoconceptual negation.

At this point the contradiction is, so to say, armed like a gun: a contradictory PAT exists which has to collapse into a predicate of P1 type or into a predicate of P2 type, which are both not contradictory.

But P1 is equivalent to empty the gun (the contradiction) extracting the bullet and assigning it to a different set from that of reference.

P2 instead empties the gun (the contradiction) shooting and sending it to increase the elements of the reference set.

In any case after the gun (the contradiction) is unloaded and the empty set has returned to be empty, that is to contain the unique deficiencies of the elements present in the reference set.

But, though the contradiction is emptied, *the state of things* (that is of the beliefs) has yet changed, as the reference set contains one more element and in the empty set there is one more deficiency.

We have already noticed that the succession of these changes of *the state of things* is isomorph to a temporal succession, where the passing of time consists of *a succession of beliefs* and not of the vain rolling of the hands of the watch.

How is the change of the state of mind (subjective) in relation to the state of things (objective)? The fact is that we do not have the knowledge of the objective state of things, but only and at the utmost the knowledge of the intersubjective state of things. That is of a knowledge where more subjectivities are convergent, probably qualified. As in the case of the scientific point of view prevailing in a time and in any case declared liable of confutation, that is *belief* as well.

CHAPTER NINE
NATURAL LANGUAGE AND FORMALIZED LANGUAGE

As Alfa and Beta's cognitive course requires also resources of knowledge which is different from personal experience, they ask themselves: "what does it mean to assert that a proposition, or a whole speech, is true?".

In the present text the natural language is almost always used, but examples or quotations of systems emerged too where a formalized language is used. Then we hint at the existing differences among the natural languages, that are those used in the spoken languages and that are then a lot and the formalized language, that can be considered unique and therefore does not need translating.

Though the natural languages are a lot, they can be reciprocally translatable.

The translation can pick up more or less well certain aesthetic characteristics of the natural languages. As a matter of fact translating texts with aesthetic characteristics, that is artistic, is art in its turn.

THE FORMALIZED LANGUAGE

Formalized language has no requisites or aesthetic pretensions and it aims instead at representing a logical structure, which is common to every natural language and it is what really makes it translatable.

Moreover the formalized language is used in particular systems, called *axiomatic-syntactical-deductive*, where some preliminary remarks are made, which should be simple and clear, that is widely sharable and from these, which are called *axioms*, they draw consequences, if possible all consequences.

Logicians and mathematicians develop their knowledge from these systems since David Hillbert (1867-1943), at the end of 1800 convinced the community of mathematicians of the opportunity to use axiomatic-deductive systems.

But the dream of a formalized language was more ancient and it can go back to Gottfried Leibnitz (1646-1716) who conceived it without realizing it (to Leibnitz and Newton we owe the differential-integral calculation, which is the language of modern physics).

A genial unlucky German Logician realized it instead Gottlob Frege (1848-1925), starting from 1879. His fundamental intuitions are valid and studied even today, though some signs he used in his calculations, are no longer current. Yet his great merits were not recognized at the beginning.

The program of formalization and of unification of the body of Mathematics was completed, after 1935 (and changing the components till the 60s), by a group of young French mathematicians, who operated under the name of *Nicolas Bourbaki*, not without goliardic reminders: it was actually the name of a French general who took part in the disastrous (for the French) French Prussian war of 1870.

The present handbooks of Mathematics reflect their reorder.

The axioms are formula, that is propositions expressed in the formal language.

From the initial formula, that is from the axioms, other formula are obtained through rules of transformation, which are the rules of formal logic. It must not be possible to derive a formula in the system and its negation because it is demonstrable that, in this case, every formula would be derivable and the system would lose every value. It would be *inconsistent*.

The fundamental point is that the development of the system happens according to *syntactic coherence*, that is according to rules which operate on the form of the language and not on its content. In the same way a match of chess takes place: the conformation of the pawnes, at a certain point of the match, depends only on applying the rules of the game. Each pawn moves according to the rules assigned and the match ends when a pawn, conventionally called "king", is eliminated by the counterpart.

Yet the axiomatic system can be interpreted and assume then a meaning. There is a theorem, said of *correctness* and *completeness*, that assures that the formula syntactically coherent, if interpreted, are *true propositions* and then semantically correct.

Then in a axiomatic deductive system the syntactic coherence generates only theorems which, once interpreted, are true propositions.

But the truth obtained in such a system is relative to the truth contained in the axioms, as the logic rules preserve and explain the truth, which was implicit in the axioms, but they do not characterize any independent truth from the axioms, and then *new*.

A new truth requires then an appropriate enlargement of the axioms.

Even a match of chess can be interpreted. In Marostica, a lovely Venetian small town, the square consists of an enormous chessboard where every two years and with living pawnes, a historical match of chess is commemorated which was played in 1454 by two knights. The winner would conquer the hand of a noble beautiful young girl, the daughter of the lord of Marostica. It was her father to choose the chess instead of swords, as then it was in use, as an intelligent son-in-law was preferred to an aggressive one. And to avoid recriminations, he committed himself to give the loser his younger daughter's hand. Apparently everybody was then happy and so every two years this happy unusual result is celebrated.

THE NATURAL LANGUAGE

But what can we say about the predicate of *truth/falsity* and of the natural language?

Alfa and Beta notice, first of all, that:

1.   Declaring a proposition false which is believed to be true constitutes a fact or declaring true a proposition which is believed false. As a matter of fact declaring true what is believed true and false what is believed false cannot modify the state of beliefs;

2.   A proposition, to be true or false, must have a meaning (a referent), as regards to this it is true or false:

3.   In general a proposition with a meaning and with an ontological value cannot refer to itself as:

a.   the proposition becomes the *individual* of whom some properties are predicated and at the same time its *predicate*, violating a fundamental law of the language: the temporal segmentation (see the following point "c");

b.   if what is predicated has a value of truth in contrast to what is attributed to the proposition, the same results true or false simultaneously, that is contradictory, as it will be clear examining the semantic paradoxes;

c.   the ontological predicates temporally segment the system of beliefs in an orderly succession, as they modify the state of beliefs. In particular the present beliefs exist, which are all thought true and the past beliefs, which are all thought false. Then an ontological proposition develops as *true-present* and constitutes the proposition it refers to in *false-past*; the conclusion is in point b);

d.   as now the future beliefs do not exist, but only the present beliefs, an ontological predicate cannot refer to *future ontological propositions* (that is, for example, to the *following proposition*) but only to a previous proposition, because only the property of *being previous* allows to be the reference of the following proposition.

Alfa and Beta notice then that every ontological proposition can be *true **or** false*.

Yet this is not everything: in the natural language every existential proposition must be *true **and** false*, though not in the same system of beliefs. And the systems of beliefs differ either because they belong to different temporal segments of the same subject or because they belong to different subjects.

But to be able to affirm that different subjects have contemporarily different beliefs a conventional time is necessary which is worth for both, as the subjective temporal successions cannot be comparable.

That is bitterly found out by the one who loves and he's not loved, the one who is in prison compared to the one who is free, the one who is ill to the one who is sound, the one who is sensitive compared to the one who is dull.

Alfa and Beta understand then what is then the inhuman function of clocks: equalizing what cannot be equalized.

Moreover Alfa and Beta understand the essential difference between a *formal-axiomatic-deductive* system, developed from a formal language, and a *system of beliefs* developed from a natural language.

From the first only theorems are derived that, if interpreted, are always true. Obviously it is necessary to accept the premises, that is the axioms of the system. As a matter of fact these are always given in such a way that they are fully acceptable. Yet, even like that, sometimes, somebody disagrees with good reasons.

From the second propositions are derived which are always *true or false* and which collapse in *only true* propositions through temporal/personal choices operated by the subjects (see chapter 8).

Then what is *true* and what is *false* are mutually relative and they even reciprocally exchange roles in the course of the development of the system of beliefs.

The disconcerting situation is that, when a PAT collapses in P 1 an P 2, a truth is eliminated, together with a contradiction: that of the others.

The natural language yet can express all this with the enormous wealth that comes from the possibility of denying every proposition. Not only the natural language can say what you want but it allows to say much more than what it is possible to say.

CHAPTER TEN
THE DISCARD

THE NATURAL LANGUAGE

Saying something implies being silent about something, Alfa and Beta learn.

Also because, even earlier, knowing something implies neglecting something else.

Then they ask themselves what the language can say and also what it cannot say.

Or better: what it must discard.

It is necessary at least to hint at what the meaning of the discard is from Alfa and Beta and in any case from every individual or cognitive system.

1)   The choice of some values implies the abandonment of other values. It is not true that it is possible to speak in any case of a choice, as the choice of the values to be achieved is also socially addressed and depends on a lot of surrounding circumstances. It depends also on genetic circumstances: sex is not chosen, neither the state of health nor the options which follow. So in the choice of values something we can define destiny comes into play, when there is nothing better.

2)   The other very general factor of discard is the discard of irrelevance. As a matter of fact Alfa and Beta are interested in *facts*, that is in what is capable to modify the state of beliefs and not in all that it confirms. Beta could say not numerable true propositions but she normally keeps silent because she adheres to the convention of discard of the irrelevance. On the other hand their senses themselves are capable of understanding the variations and of discarding the permanences.

Alfa and Beta then start learning after preventive discards, though in some cases what was discarded becomes an object of learning with the aim of a probable renewal.

When Alfa and Beta determine the collapse of PAT in P 1 or (its alternative) in P 2 they discard the contradictory proposition in opposition to the one they affirm. As it is observed in chapter 8), P 1 is a conservative choice and it discards then some potentialities. That is it discards a future of a system of beliefs. P 2 is instead a progressive choice and therefore it constitutes a past of the system of beliefs, which is P 1, and for this reason it discards that.

Yet it is clear that this is a choice of Alfa and Beta's, not of the language, which, in itself, preserves the possibility and the rightfulness to affirm all that Alfa and Beta have discarded. And even if you consider the preliminary discard at point 1) or 2), it is necessary to say that the discard concerns Alfa and Beta and not the language which preserves the possibility to express even what has been previously discarded.

The natural language can say everything and its expressive possibilities immensely exceed every concrete use, which can be made. Obviously most its surplus is made up of irrelevant contents or at least so they hope.

To understand really what the natural language discards they should meet with a different language, born from not human premises. But probably they could not understand it.

It is necessary to underline that the singular semantic power of the natural language is given by the unlimited possibility to deny every proposition and to invert its value of truth like that.

If we imagine a proposition **A** made up of the conjunctions of **n** propositions, that is something similar to a long description we have:

$A = a1 \wedge a2 \wedge a3 \wedge \ldots \wedge an;$

Let us suppose **A** is true. Then the negation of just one of the joint propositions generates a false proposition. And as we have **n** joint propositions, we have **n** ways of generating false propositions.

But obviously we can also deny the propositions *two at a time, three at a time* and finally *n at a time*.

All these propositions which have been variously denied have the same value of truth, that is they are false, yet each of them has a different meaning.

Let us ask ourselves: how many false propositions can we extract from the unique true **A** proposition.

The formula is an old acquaintance, actually the *negation* operator allows us to generate 2^n different propositions if we join **n** elementary propositions.

That is to say 8 propositions if the joint ones are 3; 16 propositions if the joint ones are 4 and so on doubling the number at every new joint proposition.

Then the number of the possible propositions grows excessively with exponential increase, but, in any case, the true proposition is always just one!

What is the result? Those who believe in the truth have to verify that the pasture of falsity are really vaster.

THE AXIOMATIC SYNTACTIC DEDUCTIVE SYSTEM

One the premises are accepted, that is the axioms, the system generates only theorems that, if interpreted, result to be real propositions. So the system is conceived to deduct only truths from their premises. Moreover the premises are clear and they can be accepted, or not, after due consideration.

It is difficult instead to accept what the premises of a proposition expressed in a natural language are, also because a part of them is implicit.

It is easy to realize that the admirable simplicity of the axiomatic-deductive system depends on the fact that it is forbidden to set premises allowing the derivation of a formula and also of its negation. In short: the obscure and vast world of falsity, where we enter through the negation, is precluded by more scrupulous creators of the one who created the natural language.

But when Leibnitz imagined that his *calculus ratiocinator* would be useful to settle human controversies peacefully, he was wrong. "Let us not quarrel – he thought – but let us sit round a table and *calculemus*".

Unfortunately true controversies are generated from differences of premises, which cannot be treated with *calculemus*.

It is still difficult to agree on simple axioms of an axiomatic system!

It is necessary to recognize that the admirable axiomatic system, as it generates only truths, does not allow differences of opinions, that, with an even excessive width, allows the natural language.

Going out of the lines we could say that the system has Soviet features.

An axiomatic system forbids, considering the natural language, also the revision of its own premises.

As a matter of fact it is a deductive system just because every formula is derived from axioms, those given and not others.

Some can be eliminated or others are given, yet, doing this, you go out of the system.

The system then is not temporally segmented, as we have verified the propositions of the natural language are, on the contrary it develops in a perfectly synchronic dimension, determined by the axioms fixing the ontology of the system and do not allow a new one.

It is then a wonderful system, but outside reality. Wonderful because outside reality.

After all it has really Soviet features.

CHAPTER ELEVEN
THE STRUCTURE OF THE LANGUAGE

THE SETS

"A set is a collection thought as a whole, of objects really distinguishable by our intuition and by our thought. The said objects are called the elements of the set".

This is the definition of the set given by Cantor, whose studies published after 1878 are the foundation of the general theory of sets and after the reorder of *Bourbaki*, of the whole Mathematics.

To form a set there are two ways:

-        Make a list of the objects of any nature which are part of it;

-        Suggest a rule which indicates what objects are part of the set.

The second way is of greater interest, as it is difficult to imagine that an arbitrary set of objects is formed.

Let us suppose to have identified, with any rule, a set of four elements and we put them between two brackets which indicate the set called A:

A = {a, b, c, d}

A with capital letter is the name of the set. Later it will be *the reference set*.

"**a, b** "… with small letters are the names of the elements. As also the sets can be elements of sets the capital/small letters of denomination has to be understood in the meaning relative to the context.

The rule of the formation of the set, which is the property the elements have in common, though they are distinguishable and distinguished from one another (like the players of one single team) is defined *intension of A*.

What the rule catches, that is the elements of the set, is defined *its extension*.

The elements are part of the set only once (that is it does not exist: {a, a, a}), intuitively, though **a** is interpreted like an object, it is the thought of an object and there are not two or more same thoughts. Actually how can we distinguish them?

The order of the set of the elements is irrelevant and that is {a, b} = {b, a}.

On the sets operations can be done with the following operators:

"∪" ; a sign of union, joining two sets and forming another which contains (one single time) the elements of the joint sets. Example: {a, c} ∪ {b, c} = {a,b,c}.

"∩" a sign of intersection which from two sets forms another containing all the elements common to the intersected sets. Example: {a,c} ∩ {b,c} = {c}

" ' " : the apex is the sign of set complementation. The complement of a set, <u>considering the reference set</u>, is a set containing all the elements of the reference set, which are not present in the first set. Example: {a,c}' = {b,d}.

If there is a relationship between a set of propositions and a set of elements (for example the propositions describe the elements), then the operators of the propositions [disjunction, conjunction and negation (V,∧ , ¬)] and the set operators [union, intersection, and complementation (∪, ∩,')] constitute **two isomorphic algebras, called of Boole** on the respective sets.

Isomorphic is a Greek term meaning *with the same shape* and, in concrete, it means that corresponding operations, executed on correspondent sets, lead to correspondent results.

Example: P (a,b) is the proposition defining the set {a,b} and P (c,d) is the proposition defining the set {c,d}. Then the proposition [P(a,b) V (P(c,d)] defines the set {a,b,c,d}, which results from the union of {a,b} ∪ {c,d}.

After this premise we can go back to the reference set {a,b,c,d} to generate all its subsets, which are exactly in correspondence to those already formed in chapter 7) examining the probabilistic predicates, or better 16 different subsets made up as follows:

1.　　　n.1 a subset made up of 4 elements and that is {a,b,c,d}, which is *the reference set A;*

2.　　　n. 4 subsets made up of 3 elements present and one absent {a, b, c , Ød}, {a,b, d, Øc}, {a, c, d, Øb }, {b, c, d, Øa};

3.　　　n. 6 subsets made up of 2 elements present and 2 missing: {a, b, Øc, Ød},.. etc;

4.　　　n.4 subsets made up of 1 element present and 3 missing: {a, Øb, Øc, Ød},... etc;

5.n. 1 subset made up of 4 missing element: {Øa, Øb, Øc, Ød}.

We notice, first of all, that the subset in point 5 does not contain any element but only deficiencies of elements and actually all the elements of the reference set are missing.

How can we interpret the set of point 5)? Let us remember the example of the poultry pen of chapter 7). If the 4 hens of the poultry pen are stolen, the poultry pen remains empty and it can be represented like an empty set, but it is always deprived of hens and not deprived of sheep, as a plundered sheep pen would be.

In short in this note the empty set is relative to the reference set and therefore it can be denominated ØA.

The Aggregate containing all the subsets of A is a set in its turn? It cannot be as in the same set there would be two incompatible elements and that is **A** and **ØA,** that constitute the presence and the lack of the same element in a set, an obviously contradictory fact. You can notice that in no subsets there are presences and deficiencies of the same elements.

We can notice again that the reference set **A** is the extension of **P (A),** that is of the property that characterizes **A**, which catches **every** existing element in the reference set, but, as one or more elements of the reference set are missing, P(A) catches one of the subsets of A. As all the elements are missing, P(A) catches the empty set **ØA.**

As the aggregate of all the subsets of A makes up the universe of the extensions that P(A) can have, we call this aggregate UrA, that is *relative Universe of the property P(A).*

UrA is *a universe of meanings of P(A),* structurally isomorph to the universe of events of chapter 7) and, as that has to collapse in a realized event, this has to collapse in a caught extension.

In UrA every subset of the reference set has its own complementary set, that is a set made up of the elements missing from the examined set (you obtain it exchanging presences with absences of elements).

Even A has a complementary set and it is ØA.

The following relationships are valid:

- A ∪ ØA = A;
- A ∩ ØA = ØA

This relationship is important because it allows us to interpret ØA as the extension of P(¬A), or as the extension of the *endoconceptual negation* we spoke about in chapter 8).

Do you remember the *not white* wedding dress?

It is right to underline that what is explained with regards to sets differs from the **theory of ZF sets** (that is formalized by the Mathematicians Zermelo and Fraenkl) for the different role of the empty set, which is unique there and it is subset of all the sets. Here instead is relative to the reference set of which it is not a subset, though a complementary set. <u>The empty set is not a subset of any set.</u>

Evidently UrA is different from the power set of A, which is foreseen in ZF as an axiom. Yet the sets contained in UrA are in a bijective mapping with the sets contained in PotA , that is in the power set of A.

(bijective mapping means: to every UrA set corresponds another in Pot A).

All this is better cleared in *L'insieme vuoto Ø: la mente* by
Lario Sinigaglia, ARMANDO EDITORE 2012.

THE STRUCTURE OF THE LANGUAGE

As we gave the premises we can now study the structure of the language, whose fundamental elements are few:

- **Individuals** who are anything that can be individualized and of whom we can predicate a property or a relationship. In this optics we consider *individuals* also the sets, the sets of sets and also the propositions. Even a *concept* is an individual, in the sense that a concept is a name given to a property when you want to identify it. <u>It can really be that the concept and the property that the concept identifies are homonymous, but it is a mistake to confound the role</u>.

- **Properties and relationships,** that is what it is predicated about the individuals. Let us ask ourselves: does a predicate always establish a relationship between an individual and a property, whose representation is an Ur, that is a relative universe (that is not a set)? No, it establishes also relationships with sets, the simplest of which is the relationship of the belonging of an element to a set containing it which is indicated with the sign "ε" (first letter of the Greek verb *estì* which means *it is)*. The sets we have spoken about till now are without a structure as this is shown by the fact that the order of their elements does not reveal.

But a predicate establishes also relationships with structured sets, on which the rational operations are possible, which are well known to us since Primary School, we will hint at that later.

Yet in no case a *property*, whose representation is an Ur, can become an *individual,* because it cannot be individualized. In reality an Ur is an aggregate of incompatible extensions and therefore it has not its own extension. Moreover the aggregate is made up of sets which are all provided with a complementary set.

Which means, remembering the isomorphism between negation (¬) in the algebra of propositions and complementation (') in the algebra of sets that every proposition regarding the elements of Ur aggregate can be denied. In short Ur is a contradictory aggregate because the property it represents is contradictory. Such contradictoriness is avoided not predicating on the property but on particular extensions of the same. That is on one of the sets contained in Ur, which is a container of sets but it is not a set.

Let us briefly hint at the structured sets.

The fundamental distinction is that between *partially ordered sets* and *totally ordered sets*.

Partially ordered sets: the elements are sometimes comparable and sometimes they are not. They can be ordered by the relationship of set inclusion "⊂" (meaning: *to be a subset*). The following image called *diagram of Hasse* makes it clearer than words the way in which the set of subsets of A = {a, b, c} is partially ordered by the set inclusion.

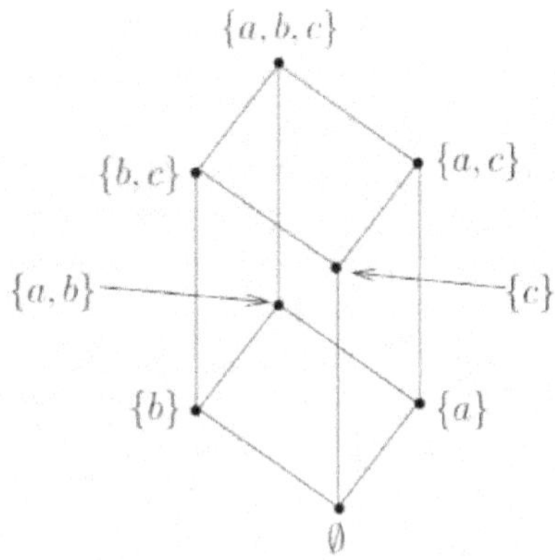

This set with the set operators (∩,∪," ′ ") is an algebric structure called **algebraic lattice** where the well-known set operations are effected.

This algebraic structure is important as every Ur aggregate is an algebraic lattice with set operators.

-        **Totally ordered sets**: the elements are always comparable and ordered by the relationship ">" e "<", meaning respectively *more than* and *less than*. The immediate examples are the dear natural numbers (1, 2, ... n) and the ordinal numbers (1°, 2° ... n°) and all the numerous sets that we order through them. They are sets totally ordered where the arithmetic operations are defined. (addition, multiplication, and so on...).

CHAPTER TWELVE
SEMANTIC PARADOXES AND SET PARADOXES

The distinction between *semantic paradoxes* and *set paradoxes* was made by the Englishman Frank Ramsey who died in 1930 at only 26 years of age. During his short life he showed an extraordinarily versatile intelligence.

The first concern the value of the truths of propositions, the second concern the existence of particular sets.

Ramsey engaged himself in the problem already pointed out in the fundamental work *Principia matematica* of Bertrand Russel and A.N. Whitehead in 1913 which intended to lay the foundations of a logical kind to Mathematics. As we know the *Bourbaki* group gave instead the foundations of the sets which are accepted today.

Ramsey's definition will be ours, after condensing in simple rules, capable of avoiding the semantic paradoxes, the considerations made previously.

SEMANTIC RULES:

1.   It is necessary that a proposition has a meaning to be *true* or *false*. Only a proposition with an ontological meaning can be true *aut* false at the same time (*aut*, a Latin conjunction which means **alternative or** indicates that the two predicates are mutually incompatible).

But in different times it can, rather it must be true *vel* false (*vel* is a Latin conjunction meaning **not alternative or**). In other words: as much a proposition can be true, as it can be false.

Tautologies are instead always true and contradictions always false.

2.   Predicates are applied only to individuals. Properties are not individuals, but they are intensions which can be represented with an **Ur** aggregate, which is contradictory, so it has no extension, nor can it be individualized. Sets, propositions

and concepts are individuals. Concepts indicate the properties, they are their names.

3.   Predicates have a dominion of individuals they can be referred to, outside which they have no meaning.

4.   The propositions are temporally segmented by the change of their value of truth. Every proposition can be denied and change the value of truth becoming contradictory, if we consider the proposition previously asserted.

5.   It is necessary to respect the order, that is the succession of the ontological predicates. Such predicates generate the semantic succession which identifies with the individual temporal succession. Consequently a proposition can refer only to a previous proposition and not to a next one, which does not exist (yet). Even less than that it can refer to itself predicating its own falsity because a paradox is the consequence.

SET RULES

1.   The set rules are reduced to a single one: the aggregate we define **Ur** (the relative universe) is not a set because it is contradictory. It represents the totality of the extensions (sets) that can potentially catch a property. Such a totality contains a number of elements which is greater than the number of the elements contained by any extension of the property, concretely caught, which we define **the reference set**. We observe that the elements of **Ur** are in bijection with those of the **power set**, which is the set of all the subsets of the reference set, in ZF theory.

Let us remember that Cantor with his fundamental **diagonal theorem** demonstrates that the power set has a greater power than that of its reference set (that is it has a greater number of elements). In particular: if the reference set contains a numerable infinity of elements, then the power set, of the reference set, contains a not numerable infinity of elements.

Then a totality, that is an Ur, which is no longer a set, if it has an infinite reference set and it is numerable, then Ur is infinite and not numerable, as you will see better later.

Cantor's diagonal theorem is an extraordinary intellectual conquest, whose structure has found fundamental applications also outside the set theory.

CHAPTER THIRTEEN
ANALYSIS OF THE PARADOXES

SEMANTIC PARADOXES: "the liar".

The paradox is generated from a proposition which cannot be classified as true or false as if *it is true, it is false* and if *it is false, it is true*.

Let us speak now about a proverbial character for those who deal with paradoxes: Epimenide from Crete, who for more than two thousand years has been in the foreground with a proposition, the consequences of which he did not consider.

Epimenide said: "all Cretans always lie".

Let us call this proposition **L**, as the liar.

Therefore if he affirms the truth, then, as he is Cretan, he affirms a falsity.

If instead he affirms a falsity, then, just because he is a liar, he might tell the truth.

Let us open a parenthesis: there is a series of witticisms of this kind: "do you know the difference between an elephant and a strawberry?".

You, who know the difference between an elephant and a strawberry very well, should say you do not know, otherwise the game does not go on.

So it is with paradoxes, you have to play the game, not because you are compliant but because they help to descend into the depths of the language.

In the case of Epimenide we should forget the fact that no liar *always lies*, because in this case, its particular semantics included, we would have a rare case of person who always tells the truth. And we should forget that even the most ruthless liar could not deny more tautological truths.

Therefore, though unlikely, we can suppose that the proposition **L** is true.

Exam of the paradox: Epidermide affirms that *all Cretans always lie*, that is *the set of the Cretans* is a subset of *the set of the liars*.

While he does not affirm *I am Cretan* because the property of *being Cretan* had been established before, so is to say.

Yet **L** proposition affirms a property of the Cretans and consequently also a property of Epimenide, as he is Cretan: that of being a liar.

Yet we are supposing that the proposition is true, while liars do not say true propositions, so Epimenide is not a liar.

Here the paradox is generated: if the proposition is true, then it is false, because Epimenide tells the truth, despite his being Cretan.

Solution of the paradox: the proposition that had previously affirmed that *Epimenide is Cretan* is implicitly falsified by the proposition which is now affirmed by Epimenide.

The conclusion is that, at the moment of the affirmation of the proposition, Epimenide is not Cretan, as he tells the truth. He was previously Cretan, according to different criteria of attribution of nationality.

We should not be amazed as we discuss about *ius sanguinis*, which means *right of the blood* that is *right of nationality derived from the parents' right* and about *ius soli,* meaning *the right of the soil* and then *right of nationality dependent on the place of birth.* It is not a novelty: it has been discussed since the time of Greek *polis*.

We incidentally notice that every legal system functions like that: successive laws can implicitly abrogate previous laws. And, obviously this works also for the language, one just has to take notes.

Let us suppose that **L** is false.

In this case the solution is easy: it is not true that all the Cretans lie, but at least just one lies: our Epimenide, precisely.

You should notice that not all the autoreferential propositions are paradoxical, but those that are affected by an internal semantic contrast, like the one examined here.

And the paradox itself points out that the proposition is not correct. Therefore we should refuse it specifically, like those who see that a part of the food is rotten and throws it away, keeping the wholesome part.

SEMANTIC PARADOXES: Grelling-Nelson's paradox.

The adjectives (the properties) of the language have to be divided into two categories:

- We define *autological* adjectives those which refer to themselves.

Example: *polisyllabic* is an adjective which refers to itself as the word polysyllabic has more than one syllable.

- We define *eterological* adjective those which do not refer to themselves.

Example: *monosyllabic* does not refer to itself because the word *monosyllabic* has more than one syllable.

Here is the paradox: *eterological* (subject), whenever it had the property of being *eterological* (predicate), then it would be *autological*; that is, if it would not refer to itself, then it would refer just to itself. Such is the meaning of *eterological*.

Instead if *eterological* (subject) had the property of being *autological* (predicate), than it would be *eterological*.

In conclusion the property *eterological* seems to belong to both categories, into which the properties had been divided, though each property is the negation of the other and then there would be a contradiction.

Solution of the paradox:

1. In particular the example with the property *polysyllabic* is not pertinent. It is the word that appoints the property, that has the property of being polysyllabic and not the property itself, which could be appointed by a monosyllabic word;

2.   In general: 1°: the properties are all *eterological*, that is they refer to individuals and not to themselves. Then there are no *autological* properties; 2°a property is not an individual and then it cannot serve as an individual variable.

It is then a case of pathological autoreference which is moreover realized with incorrect premises.

SEMANTIC PARADOXES: "the crossed reference"

"the following sentence is true";

"the sentence which comes before is false".

Paradox: let us suppose the first sentence is true, then also the following sentence is true. But it tells that the first sentence is false, against the hypothesis.

Then let us suppose the first sentence is false. Then the second sentence is false. In this case the first sentence is true against the hypothesis.

Solution of the paradox: the propositions which bear ontological predicates (like those of the example) form a well ordered succession (for the reasons seen previously) and they cannot then determine vicious circularity. The predicate of *truth/falsity* is always ontological when it inverts the truth value of a previous, *but it cannot invert the value of truth of a following sentence.*

We notice then that the paradoxes point automatically at the abuses of the language and this wisdom of the language is a further reason of amazement: it seems an instrument and it is instead more intelligent than us.

It would be as if, within the law, the person who commits a crime would denounce himself for internal constriction.

SEMANTIC PARADOXES: "the reinforced liar".

The paradoxes called of the *reinforced liar* are a lot and they are the result of the work of giving a hand to Epimenide to abuse the language. For example the following:

Proposition: "now I am lying"

Paradox:

-       if the sentence is true then it is false, because it affirms to be a lie;

-       if a sentence is false, then its negation is true, that is *I am not lying*; but as the sentence is false, then its meaning is against the hypothesis made.

It is a pathological selfreference: as a matter of fact the meaning of the affirmation *I am lying* is in contrast with the value of truth that the sentence implicitly attributes to itself, that is of being false. But if the sentence is false, then *I am not lying*, then the sentence is true. But if the sentence is true then *I am lying*, then the sentence is false. We notice how the autoreference obliges to a vicious semantic circle. It is an abuse of the language.

SET PARADOXES: "the contradictory totalities"

We deal with sets because they allow us to clarify of what *being a property* really consists.

The paradoxes, but it would be better to define them *contradictions*, are generated from the fact that the **totalities**, both finite and infinite, cannot be sets for already anticipated reasons and which we now resume.

Let us start to observe that every set is the extension of an intension and this last one is the property defining the elements of the set. Each element of the set has a general property, called **P** in force of which it is the element of the set, named **A**, and a particular property, which distinguishes it from the other elements of the **A** set.

An isomorphism exists, already examined in chapter 11) between the algebra of the set and the algebra of the propositions, consequently the logical operations made on the propositions, using the logical connectives *conjunctions, disjunctions and negation* ($\wedge$, $\vee$, $\neg$) are isomorphic , that is they have the same form of the set operations made on the

extensions of the propositions, using the operators *intersections, union and complementation* (∩, ∪, ').
Now here there are: { a, b, c } the elements of the **A** set or better the extension of **P** property.
In **A** there is every existent element, which has **P** property.
Can we also say that in **A** there is the totality of the elements that have **P** property (or better all the possible elements that have P property)?
We cannot say that, because certainly **P** property belongs also to every subset of **A** and therefore to each of the elements of the set of all the subsets of A, that in the theory of the ZF sets (formalized by Zermelo and Fraenkel) is called *power set* of the reference set, that is of A and here called **PotA**.
(Please do not confound *PotA* with *pota* of chapter 5).
The power set of A, that is PotA, has n. 8 elements, as we already know.
Let us now interpret the Ø empty set (which is unique in ZF and is a subset of every set) in a relative sense, that is indicating the lack of a definite element. Therefore **Øa** indicates, in a set, the lack of the **a** element and we build **Ur of A**, with the modalities considered in chapter 7.
The elements of UrA are in a bijective mapping with those of PotA.
We notice that in PotA every x element is such that: **x ∈ UrA,** is different from any other and every element has its own complementary set compared with A, that is **x'**,
containing every element of A which is not contained in **x** and without every element of A contained in **x**.
For this reason the proposition **P (x)**, describing the x element and the **P(x')** proposition describing the **x'** element, in an algebra of propositions, are one the negation of the other. There are then the following relationships **among propositions**:
$P(x) \wedge P(x') \equiv P(\text{Ø}A) \equiv P(\text{Ø}a, \text{Ø}b, \text{Ø}c) \equiv P(\neg A);$
$P(x) \vee P(x') \equiv P(A) \equiv P(a, b, c)$ and then

P(A) ≡ ¬ P(ØA) ≡ ¬P(¬A);
Yet both the propositions, P(A) e P(¬A), describe the elements of UrA
("≡" put between two propositions means: *the two propositions have the same meaning and can be reciprocally substituted*).
These relationships show that in UrA there is the extension of all the propositions which define sets with P property and therefore UrA contains the extension of every P(x) proposition and also of every P(¬ x) proposition and in particular UrA contains A and ØA at the same time, that is to say that it contains both the A element and the lack of A element.
This is a contradiction, allowed in Ur, which is an aggregate explicitly contradictory, but it is not allowed in any set.
For this reason no set can contain the totality of the elements with P property, but a set can contain every (existing) element with P property.
In other words P property has some potentialities which define elements exceeding the possibility of coexistence of the elements themselves. In particular: if A element exists, then ØA does not exist.
A, that is the reference set, represents the utmost opportunity of coexistence of the elements of UrA and also the maximum not contradictory extension of P.
There are the following relationships:
1)   U(UrA) = {a, b, c} = A
2)   ∩ (UrA) = {Øa ; Øb ; Øc } = ØA
(UX e ∩X are respectively the operators *generalized union of the elements of the sets of X and generalized intersection of the elements of the sets of X* with an intuitive meaning).
The relationships 1) and 2) formally exhibit what was formed previously and that is that A represents the maximum possibility of coexistence of elements of sets of UrA.

FINITE TOTALITIES AND INFINITE TOTALITIES

An infinite set cannot be described through enumerations of its elements and therefore it exists as far as the law supplying its elements exists, one by one and distinctively.

A law similar to the one that generates, one by one, the elements of the infinite set generated through the axiom of infinity of ZF theory, which can be interpreted like the well-known natural numbers (1,2,3 ….n) whose elements are obviously numerable, that is they can be counted, like those of any set corresponding to it

(example an amount of money)

We notice that every element of the set, that is every natural number, is in turn a set.

Even this set has its own power set, and a fundamental theorem of Cantor shows that the elements of this set are not numerable (intuitionally they cannot be counted because they are a lot more than the numbers).

After these premises, let us consider the so called set paradoxes, mentioning just one because every other has got the shape of this:

-        Paradox of Cantor: ***The set of all sets*** *cannot exist, as its power set would have a greater number of elements of the same, which is obviously contradictory.*

Suggested solution of the paradox: *being a set* is clearly a property.

But it is doubtful that it can be a property of ZF set where, starting from $\emptyset$, the empty set, every object of ZF is a set. If a property is not defining, it is not a property.

The situation in the interpretation of the empty set is really different as it is a deficiency relative to the reference set.

Let us define **NAST**, that is **natural set theory**, the system where *the empty set is not absolutely empty, but relatively empty.* In such interpretation, all the elements of the reference set are missing in the empty set. Therefore such an empty set is different from an empty set, that has another reference set.

Such a set, which is empty if compared to the reference set, is part of aggregate Ur, built with known modalities, starting from the reference set itself.

An Ur is the aggregate of the possible extensions of a property (like P in the previous example) and that is the aggregate containing all the subsets of the reference set (like A in the previous example) and moreover *it contains the empty set*. We have to remember that *in NAST the empty set is not the subset of any set*, but it is the complementary set of the reference set. Therefore only Ur contains the empty set.

*Then in **NAST** not everything is a **set** because the **Ur** exist.*

The individuals exist too, who are the elements of the sets, yet we have already explained that the difference between a set and an element of set is relative to the context. As a matter of fact the sets can be the elements of other sets. In short elements and sets are not structurally different. <u>Yet the sets and the Ur are instead different: **as a matter of fact in no set and in all Ur there is the empty set**</u>.

This opposition illuminates the structural distinction between *individuals/sets and properties* you find in chapter 11 in the paragraph "Structure of the language". **Actually what makes properties different from every individual/set is the ability to catch the empty set.**

NAST, that is *natural set theory*, is, in our opinion, the set system that human beings and probably superior animals use naturally, our brothers with *four hands* and *four legs*.

Going back to Cantor's Paradox the solution suggested in NAST is that the set of all sets, as it is the totality of a property **P (I)** (that is the property of being a set), is equivalent to **Ur(I),** an aggregate that is not a set and that would be in bijective mapping with the power set of the dominion of individuals made up of sets. This last is the reference set of the property **P(I),** that is the extension of the property of **being a set**.

If *being a set* is a property defining in ZF, something we doubt. Moreover as in NAST the empty set catches *every element missing in the reference set,* you can easily foresee *those only potentially missing in the reference set.* And as the elements potentially missing can really be infinite, *then every Ur is an aggregate which is potentially not numerable.* **In fact, only the Ur are not numerable, while every set, if infinite, is numerable**.

Then in the opposition between *individuals/sets* and *properties,* in our opinion, the fundamental opposition between *continuous* and *discontinuous* is evident. An opposition which, in our opinion is irreducible.

The subject is fascinating and you can deepen it on "Complimentary in Mathematics. A first introduction to fhe Foundations of Mathematics and its History" by Willelm Kuyk, Reidel Publishing Company, Dordrecht 1977.

Finito di stampare nel mese di Novembre 2015
per conto di Youcanprint *Self - Publishing*